Allen Ginsberg

THE LATE GREAT

Allen Ginsberg
THE LATE GREAT

A PHOTO BIOGRAPHY

Christopher Felver

Eulogy by **Lawrence Ferlinghetti** & In Memory of Allen by **David Shapiro**

Pictograms by Neeli Cherkovski & Christopher Felver

Thunder's Mouth Press | **New York**

THE LATE GREAT ALLEN GINSBERG: A Photo Biography

© 2002 by Christopher Felver

Published by
Thunder's Mouth Press
An Imprint of Avalon Publishing Group Incorporated
161 William St., 16th Floor
New York, NY 10038

Library of Congress Cataloging-in-Publication Data

Felver, Christopher, 1946-
    The Late Great Allen Ginsberg: a photo biography / by Christopher Felver
        p. cm.
    ISBN 1-56025-382-7 (tradepaper)
        1. Ginsberg, Allen, 1926--Pictorial works. 2. Poets, American—20th
century--Biography--Pictorial works. 3. Beat generation—Pictorial works. I. Title.
    PS3513.I74 Z6 2002
    811'.54--dc21
    [B]   2002024396
            ISBN 1-56025-382-7

        9   8   7   6   5   4   3   2   1

Cover: The Buddhist Jew with a Tibetan lama's mindful soul contemplates the
brevity of epic poetry and the endlessness of haiku.

Page ii: Allen Ginsberg and his Beat colleagues shared a fascination with Far Eastern thought. Ginsberg's
Buddhist mudra, offered after hot water and lemon at the Caffe Trieste in North Beach,
makes perfect sense. This coffeehouse was Ginsberg's morning headquarters in San Francisco. 1981

Designed by Susi Oberhelman
Printed in the United States of America
Distributed by Publishers Group West

"So this is the
Forest of Arden!"
— w.s.

Allen Ginsberg
July 29, 1981

A Division of Nalanda Foundation, a Non-Profit Educational Corporation.

I hear America singing, the varied carols I hear...
Singing with open mouths their strong melodious songs.

WALT WHITMAN

I Hear America Singing 1860

Acknowledgments

Master prints: Kirk Anspach, David Spindler
Photographic support: Alex Ivanov
Editorial Assistance: Eva Reitspiesova, Bill Norton
Captions Editor: Joyce Jenkins
Special thanks: Lawrence Ferlinghetti, John Yau,
Bill Morgan, Rita Bottoms, Anthony Bliss,
Bill McPheron, Rodney Phillips, Susan Johnson,
Douglas Brinkley, David Amram, Allan Woll, Rick DePofi

Introduction

by Christopher Felver

The first image I saw of Allen Ginsberg was in issue number two of *Evergreen Review* (1957), devoted to San Francisco poets. The works of these emerging subversive talents were accompanied by Harry Redl's photographic portraits that captured the exuberance of the West Coast literary scene. These hot shots of bohemia fascinated me.

Everybody knows that Allen Ginsberg was a major mover and shaker in the Beat movement, East and West. In 1966, Ginsberg organized a benefit for Cleveland poet d.a. levy's defense fund. *Cleveland: The Rectal Eye Vision*, levy's book, offended Cleveland authorities and he was charged with obscenity. When Ginsberg and his cohorts came from New York to levy's rescue, I learned how writers tend to look out for one another. I personally had to face the draft in 1968, and it was then that I saw a news photo of Jean Genet, Terry Southern, William Burroughs, and Ginsberg at the Democratic convention in Chicago. Ginsberg's cool anti-war stance made him a seminal voice for those of us who didn't accept the deadly involvement of the U.S. in Southeast Asia. The determination of this group of artists to change the status quo inspired me to read all I could about them.

I finally met Ginsberg in 1979 in San Francisco's City Lights Bookstore, where Lawrence Ferlinghetti published the visionary *Howl and Other Poems*. Neeli Cherkovski and Raymond Foye arranged a benefit reading for the twentieth anniversary of *Beatitude* magazine, and Ginsberg flew in for it. He seemed to know or be known by everyone. He performed William Blake's "The Tyger" with his harmonium, and Peter Orlovsky joined him with vocals and banjo. Poets Joanne Kyger, Bob Kaufman, Howard Hart, Michael McClure, Gregory Corso, and Lawrence Ferlinghetti also read. The overflow crowd prompted a second show the same night. The Buddhist ethic in Jack Kerouac's *Desolation Angels* was operating that night in North Beach—a central idea of Dharma being to be compassionate and open. Allen Ginsberg exemplified this ideal. That evening swept me into the world of literary San Francisco. Standing offstage during the performances, I made the initial photographs in this collection.

The following summer, Gregory Corso invited me to his class at Naropa Institute in Boulder, Colorado. I called Ginsberg, who had co-founded the Jack Kerouac School of Disembodied Poetics there. He said, "If you're not a cop, then come on up." I borrowed a van, drove to Boulder, and slept for a night at the bottom of the stairs of the house that Ginsberg and Orlovsky had rented. In the morning Peter was "hummin' an' a dustin' " around the house, keeping the kitchen shining clean. Allen was in the living room expounding on Walt Whitman's ecstatic naked multitudinous truth while he prepared for class.

In 1982, Naropa sponsored a twenty-fifth anniversary celebration of the publication of Kerouac's *On the Road*. Organized and emceed by Ginsberg, it featured poetry and prose readings, art exhibits, film screenings, and parties. Poets, scholars, hangers-on, and Beat aficionados came from everywhere. This reunion was a testament to the achievements of the new American writing.

In 1985, I moved to Macdougal Street in Greenwich Village. I visited Ginsberg in his busy East Village pad, just around the corner from St. Mark's Church. One night he offered to exchange photographs: his haunting image of Gregory Corso in the attic of the Beat Hotel in Paris for my portrait of Isamu Noguchi in Long Island City. After that, Ginsberg always clued me in to his doings and made sure my name appeared on his guest lists. I saw him often while I was finishing my book, *The Poet Exposed*. Allen's generosity became the model for me to always give back whenever possible.

In the activity of the Beats in the following years, Ginsberg was usually at its center. The art world buzzed as curators staged major Beat retrospectives during the mid-1990's. In 1994, New York University sponsored a major conference on the Beats, including a "Beat Art" exhibition at the Washington Square East Gallery. Another show, "Beat Culture and the New America: 1950–1965" traveled from the Whitney Museum of American Art to the Walker Art Center in Minneapolis and the de Young Museum in San Francisco. The Beats had finally been legitimized by American culture—and, in the end, on their own terms.

The last time I saw Allen Ginsberg was at City Lights, on what was to be his final visit to San Francisco. He had come for lunch with Ferlinghetti. I remember that when we first met, Ginsberg's ties and wide-lapel jackets had come from thrift shops. Now, dressed in a designer suit (still bought in a second hand store) and elegant scarf, he seemed to have grown into the clothes of a member of the Academy of Arts and Letters. Heading up Columbus Avenue, Allen walked with his hands clasped behind his back, like a rabbi in contemplation, and I could tell that he was slowing down. I felt he had returned to San Francisco to contemplate the magic of the early years when all possibilities were there for the taking.

What I treasure most is Ginsberg's turning me on to John Keats' idea of "negative capability." It's exactly that need to understand the opposite perspective, all sides of an issue—to be receptive to the whole picture—that made me a better photographer. It helped me realize what it was to be photographed, and to understand the sudden fusion of identities that occurs in the mysterious openness between photographer and subject.

SAN FRANCISCO 2002

In Memory of Allen

by David Shapiro

In memory of Kenneth Koch

I remember seeing Allen before I saw him—early photographs of the "Beats" when I was, say, 10 years old, brought back from San Francisco by a dentist's son, who sported a beard and had subtle things to say about Ferlinghetti and how the repetitions of Death could sound with difference.

I remember becoming Allen at 12-year-olds' parties. I played a set of bongo drums and made an idiot of myself as I recited in the rain. Because of these early imitations—a break away from more usual Roethke or Eliot imitations—my eighth grade yearbook is filled with signatures that read: "To the Beat Prophet." I memorized as much of Allen as I could find in Don Allens' *New American Poetry 1945-1960* and at the Gotham Book Mart, where Rimbaud and the Symbolists had already transformed my young violinist's life.

In Weequahic High School, Allen's Aunt Honey (Litzky) read me letters from Allen. She adored Allen, and she was an intelligent reciter of Stephen Crane, another Newark poet. I loved her and kept in touch through the years. She would speak reverently of his journeys through India. She told me not to stay in her class but to go simply to the library upstairs for a year and read.

I remember wanting to meet Allen desperately. Frank O'Hara "set up" a meeting at his loft. Allen first intimidated me by silently stalking the bookshelves. After a very long time waiting for him to address me, he said: "Are you a virgin?" One forgets the answer. He told me my poetry was too abstract and that I should write about my beautiful green sweater. I remonstrated that I didn't want to write about my beautiful green sweater. He later wrote to me that I should write about local pathetic grocery boys. I didn't want to but I wrote 100 sonnets and many about local incidents. I resented him. He chanted for almost an hour, and I resented that. I played *Nigun* by Bloch, and he asked me if I had improvised it. I told him the title meant Improvisation. I thought he would be young and flashing and insolent as Rimbaud. I found him warm and pudgy and thorny.

I remember taking Allen for a walk around Weequahic Lake. I told him that I had seen God when I was five and that He had worn pants up to the tallest waves and predicted that the bulwarks would be destroyed. Allen said: "Ah, the destruction of the bulwarks at Deal!" I always loved that phrase. I reminded him that he too had seen visions, but Allen said he was a little skeptical of them. I praised Ashbery, and he asked whether the poems were capable of being memorized. I was proud to show him that I could recite an hour of Ashbery, including the cubo-futurist ending of "Rain" from *The Tennis Court Oath*. When I finished, he said: "Now I get it—it's like Alexander Pope." I was disappointed by this analogy, but I heard later that he felt my recitation had helped him understand John's poetry.

I remember Allen always telling me he didn't understand my poetry. I later told him that I didn't believe that. I told him that I had thought of writing him an angry letter—this was years later, perhaps even in my forties—but that the theme, that he delighted in his imitators and was positive toward other styles—seemed inappropriately Oedipal. I told him that I had decided that he was fine just the way he was and that I wouldn't annoy him with that kind of screed. He smiled and very genially said "Thank you." I remember being so moved by a sentence in which Allen said that he would always regret not having been sweeter to certain aging uncles. I told him that I thought this the height of Jewish prudential wisdom, as is said of Freud by Marcus on the subject of unhappy money, and that I would use this advice to visit as much as possible.

Though Stein said, "There is never all of any visit," I always remembered this part of Allen.

I remember walking around the Park in the early 60s with Allen, and I praised *Howl* and *Kaddish*, and he said he was producing another book but they were hard acts to follow. He saw some men smoking and asked for a cigarette. He told me, of these black men, "That is the true masculine rhythm of America, David." I told him they seemed very angry at him and were possibly unemployed and enraged. We vacillated in conversation about who would play the vatic and who would play the realist. When Frank O'Hara was killed in 1966, I was weeping at the funeral and enraged with Frank Lima at the priest, who had, we thought, insulted Frank as a naughty boy like Bobby Burns, etc. Allen saw me and said: "Don't worry, you won't die." Also: "Frank is alive somewhere." And I thought: No, he isn't. But later, I thought it poignant that he had tried to console us.

I remember Allen taking photographs at the National Academy. He dressed well and so did Gary Snyder. I cajoled him to take a photograph of myself. He did, but I was ashamed of asking. I recall how well he sat on TV while Elaine deKooning painted him almost instantly. I remember that when I was a bit angry, at the Nova Convention, with the melodrama of the artists, Allen listened and later read a very quiet love poem and told me it was a response to what I had said. This was the Buberian in Allen, that we had indeed met. My little sister felt that he could not quite place her, ever, but I was always dazzled by how many swam inside his consciousness, as when, at our last reading at Columbia, just a year or so before his death, a monsignor of the Church attended and I thought I would be happy in making an introduction. Instead, Allen swiftly turned and said: "Oh, hello, Pierre," as if no city could contain his aficionados.

I remember when Allen came to my class at Brooklyn College. The kids were mesmerized by him and Peter. Allen, I thought, would just be a celebrity and difficult or nerve-wracking. Instead, he did all the assignments in class. One he said he loved was "to treat an object without contempt." Peter wrote as beautifully as a saint. Allen wrote a poem that was published, "Brooklyn College Brain," which stunned me with its particularity. The "snapshot" aesthetic, which at least one critic has used against Frank O'Hara, was here adumbrated in a simple Hello and Goodbye formula.

I remember seeing Allen in Paris with his father and stepmother, say 1967. Allen moved through the streets and was often recognized and gentle in response. He paid homage to George Whitman, where I was staying, as part of an improvised student hostel. Allen and his father were making up, as it were, and since I had known about the family mood and resentments—Aunt Honey had lamented all schisms—I was moved by Allen's gentle treatment of his father. Louis made jokes in the Louvre about the Venus: "Greatest case of disarmament in the world." Allen seemed ashamed and moved to one side of a Fra Angelico and gave me his wisdom about LSD. He took his father to one of the bridges and recited the Pont Mirabeau poem. I remonstrated lightly that the bridge was not Mirabeau. He shooshed me in a very Jewish way, muttering: 'Let the old man enjoy it!" I thought this was the height of Jewish filial devotion and I have never forgotten it.

I remember Allen and his melodies. I remember him squeezing the box at readings and delighting me with what came of his seemingly doomed attempts to set Blake. I remember my doomed friend of the Fugs, the flutist and composer Lee Crabtree, who felt that Allen was a good businessman and being difficult about rights.

I remember thinking that certain poets were just imitating Allen with a serape. I remember being teased by Allen as a "crypto-heterosexual" and patiently explaining my gender choices to him. He was never aggressive. I remember asking him how he could put up with my old teacher Chogyam and his absolutes. He told me: "I'm a masochist, David."

I remember Allen telling me that my best poems had been those written with my sister. This seemed an opaque insult, but later I thought it very percipient, since the whole rage for children's work was in part something he could truly understand. He preferred simplicity. He told me, "You write with your head and maybe heart, but I write also with my cock." I remember when he used the phrase "fucking in the dust" with my mother in 1964 or so, she was charmed, and I told her she was not being coherent with her usual rules. "It's different when he uses those words," she averred, and Kenneth (Koch) once said in class that very few poets could get away with certain words as Allen did.

I remember thinking at Allen's memorial that it would be good to play a Jewish song, because Allen, while always calling himself a Buddhist, was my ideal of the Jewish cantor. They are wrong who say that *Kaddish* is not a good Jewish poem. It is one of the best of the last 50 years, and it is not for nothing that Jasper Johns went twice to hear *Kaddish* with sets by Eric Fischl. Allen's wounding poem has been deposed because *Kaddish* is not, it is said, a lament for the dead. I note, however, that anyone in the Jewish community knows that Kaddish is indeed, among other things, associated with our rituals of mourning. Wieseltier's *Kaddish* was written in the year of his father's death. I am astonished by those who do not find in that poem the realist thickness and the domestic thickness that makes it as good as any drama by Miller or novel by both Roths.

I remember giving Allen a copper plate and asking him to draw on it, like his beloved Blake. He did. He was ready with gifts. He gave me FBI files in the 70s to show me how the New Left had been infiltrated.

We spoke of Clemente and the new young painters who adored him. I played Achron's *Hebrew Melody* at his funeral or memorial or celebration, let us call it, at St Mark's. Though the violin was not my own, though it was a strange and unlovely time in many ways, I performed it, as I often had for Allen, as if it were my Bar Mitzvah. He deserved an impeccable performance, because he was much more than we who knew him too well had thought. He had decided, he told me, to teach breathing at Brooklyn College. It was something that he knew.

I remember Lou Asekoff of Brooklyn College telling someone that he was still learning from Allen after his death. I remember telling Allen that one rich family had told me they would give him money, but that he would squander it on his friends. He told me that I should tell them he was not going to do that, but it was normal that he called friends before his death and asked them if they needed anything. It was normal for Allen to be understood by many, instantaneously as a martyr in Prague, King of the May, as when at Rattner's a waiter sidled up to us and said, in peccable accents, "Keep up the good works, Allen." Like President Havel, he was a restoration of sanity in a time of dogmas. He is in the anthologies by now, but for us he will be always more, more Tolstoyan, more genial, more muscular too, because we have known him before and after the anthologies. I still remember Allen at an opening at Michael Goldberg's loft, once Rothko's, and as Peter O.

agitated the dishes and utensils in the sink like one on fire, Allen cried: "This party lacks a true gaiety!"

I remember the true happiness in Allen, who charmed even the great Kabbalist Scholem and his wife. And who charmed my mother, and who charmed the universe with more than a great soul. He was a worker, and I admired a dream-entry he made of a walk with Kissinger. He was "one of the workers," and it is not for nothing that Chris Felver has luckily given us his naked face. My wife said how lucky Chris was to be there and see the community of poets, but it is not luck, anymore than my having sent a student to get my Whitman inscribed by Allen. The world used him, and he used the world, and he apparently had the easiness of Mayakovsky in doing so early and late. His taste was questionable to some, but he had a tolerance for chaos that made him a true artist. I will not list here my favorite poems for the canon. I will just remember his asymmetrical face, marred one might say by his bout with one nervous disorder, and the Socratic beauty that was generated by his Silenus-like glimmer and empathy. How angry he was that Trilling had died in pain! How much more sympathetic than Trilling himself in his story of the young Allen. How much a comrade he was to me as he listened to my kidney-stone problems and told me about his wilder solutions. It is not for nothing that when he told my teacher, Meyer Schapiro, that he had been jailed, that Meyer cheered him with a story of his own incarceration. These two, the great scholar and the great poet, were united in their love of freedom and justice, discovered, after all, in the great art of the human portrait.

NEW YORK CITY 2002
David Shapiro, poet and art critic

Allen in Person

by Lawrence Ferlinghetti

He is one of the prophets come back
He is one of the wiggy prophets come back
He had a beard in the Old Testament
        but shaved it off in Paterson
He has a microphone around his neck
        at a poetry reading
        and he is more than one poet
        and he is an old man perpetually writing a poem
        about an old man
        whose every third thought is Death
        and who is writing a poem
        about an old man
        whose every third thought is Death
        and who is writing a poem
        Like the picture on a Quaker Oats box
        that shows a figure holding up a box
        upon which is a picture of a figure
        holding up a box
        and the figure smaller and smaller
        and further away each time
        a picture of shrinking reality itself
He is one of the prophets come back
        to see to hear to file a revised report
        on the present state
        of the shrinking world
He has buttonhooks in his eyes
        with which he fastens on
        to every foot of existence
        and onto every shoestring rumor
        of the nature of reality
        And his eye fixes itself
        on every stray person or thing
        and waits for it to move
        like a cat with a dead white mouse
        suspecting it of hiding

some small clew to existence
and he waits gently
for it to reveal itself
or herself or himself
and he is gentle as the lamb of God
made into mad cutlets
And he picks up every suspicious object
and he picks up every person or thing
examining it and shaking it
like a white mouse with a piece of string
who thinks the thing is alive
and shakes it to speak
and shakes it alive
and shakes it to speak
He is a cat who creeps at night
and sleeps his buddhahood in the violet hour
and listens for the sound of three hands
about to clap
and reads the script of his brainpan
his hieroglyph of existence
He is talking asshole on a stick
he is a walkie-talkie on two legs
and he holds his phone to his ear
and he holds his phone to his mouth
and he speaks with an animal tongue
and man has devised a language
that no other animal understands
and his tongue sees and his tongue speaks
and his own ear hears what is said
and clings to his head
He is a forked root walking
with a knot-hole eye in the middle of his head
and his eye turns outward and inward
and sees and is mad
and is mad and sees

And he is the mad eye of the fourth person singular
of which nobody speaks
and he is the voice of the fourth person singular
in which nobody speaks
and which yet exists
with a long head and a foolscap face
and the long mad hair of death
of which nobody speaks
And he speaks of himself and he speaks of the dead
of his dead mother and his Aunt Rose
with their long hair and their long nails
that grow and grow
and they come back in his speech without
a manicure
And he has come back with his black hair
and his black eye and his black shoes
and the big black book of his report
And he is a big black bird with one foot raised
to hear the sound of life reveal itself
on the shell of his sensorium
and he speaks to sing to get out of his skin
and he pecks with his tongue on the shell of it
and he knocks with his eye on the shell
For he is a head with a head's vision
and his is the lizard's look
and his unbuttoned vision is the door
in which he stands and waits and hears
And he is his own ecstatic illumination
and he is his own hallucination
and he is his own shrinker
and his eye turns in the shrinking head of the world
For he has come at the end of the world
and he is the flippy flesh made word
and he is his own last word
and his own last word is Love

▲ **Local poets congregated** whenever Ginsberg came to North Beach in the 1970s and 1980s. Standing, left to right: translator/editor George Scrivani, poet/biographer Neeli Cherkovski, Allen, Lawrence, Kerouac biographer Gerald Nicosia, and poet Jack Mueller. Kneeling, left to right: unidentified, Swiss artist Matteus Pfaff, and Beat photographer Mark Green. 1980

◀ **By publishing** *Howl,* City Lights Books put the Beat Generation on the map. Ginsberg, Lawrence Ferlinghetti, and co-editor Nancy Peters jam the front door to City Lights Bookstore, which Ferlinghetti always saw as a "kind of library where books are sold." 1981

◀ **"San Francisco...It's one hell of a Paris,"** Charles Bukowski sardonically remarked. Ferlinghetti sits in the now long-gone Cafe Americain with Ginsberg. Both were true denizens of North Beach's cafe society, a neighborhood that Ferlinghetti calls "The Casbah." 1980

▶ **"I want people to bow** as they see me and say he is gifted with poetry,/ he has seen the presence of the Creator."— Allen Ginsberg, from "Transcription of Organ Music." 1980

▲ **Meeting Beat poet Bob Kaufman**—who declared "Thank God for Beatniks"—at City Lights. Kaufman, who was known in France at "The American Rimbaud," often proclaimed to the habitues of the Caffe Trieste, "Allen Ginsberg is King." 1980

◀ **On a chilly morning in North Beach** with Neeli Cherkovski. Cherkovski profiled Ginsberg in *Whitman's Wild Children*, which begins: "The first thing Allen Ginsberg ever said to me was 'You're fat.' I answered: 'And you're bald.'" 1980

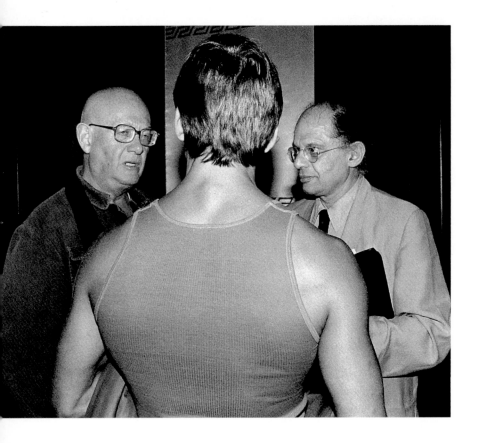

◄ **Zen priest Philip Whalen** at a San
Francisco Zen Center poetry reading.
Ginsberg hailed Whalen as a true "poet's
poet." Whalen, Gary Snyder and Lew
Welch attended Reed College in Portland
together, later filtering down to San
Francisco; Whalen's collection of poems,
On Bear's Head, is a classic. 1980

▶ **Students surround Michael McClure** and Ginsberg backstage at the Zen
Center reading. Allen had already penned his "Don't Smoke" mantra against
the tobacco industry, but still gave in to the nicotine gods from time to time. 1980

▲ ***Beatitude* magazine's** 20th anniversary reading held at the Savoy Tivoli in North Beach. The event drew more than 500 people, including then-Governor Jerry Brown. *Beatitude* was co-founded by Bob Kaufman and Lawrence Ferlinghetti to give voice to the unspoken and the unspeakable. 1979

▶ **Peter Orlovsky, poet and life companion** to Allen, often joined him onstage with voice and banjo. 1979

▶ **"I never go to heaven,** Nirvana, X, Whatchamacallit, I never left Earth,/ I never learned to die."—Allen Ginsberg, from "Ode to Failure." 1979

◀ **While earning a doctorate** in music from Brown University, longtime collaborator Steven Taylor set many of Ginsberg's poems to music, including "Capital Air." 1979

▲ **Peter Orlovsky appears in many** of Ginsberg's poems. They collaborated on *Straight Hearts' Delight, Love Poems and Selected Letters, 1947-1980.* 1981

◀ **Peter Orlovsky on the balcony** of their "home away from home" at the University Apartments in Boulder during Naropa's summer poetics session. 1981

▲ **Gregory Corso flanked by two old friends.** The Villon-like Corso also claimed Shelley as a literary soulmate. Gregory met Allen in 1950 in Manhattan—the beginning of a madcap friendship in life, poetry, and nonstop travel. 1981.

◀ **Before class and students** on a busy Naropa day, Peter helps Allen plan an upcoming reading tour. 1980

▶ **Going over proof sheets** for an exhibition at Holly Solomon's gallery in New York City. Ginsberg began documenting his companions in the early 1940s, using an old Leica and sharing results with photographers Robert Frank, Elsa Dorfman, and Berenice Abbott. 1980

▲ **Gregory wrestles Allen** for either money or a momentary gain in conversation. No matter how they argued, or how boisterous the exchange, Ginsberg always left bemused by the unquenchable life force of his pal. 1980

▲ **A New Yorker with a car cleans the windshield** of his old Volvo. From Kerouac in *On the Road* to Burroughs in *Junky*, cars loom large in the Beat cosmology. As Ginsberg put it in his 1953 poem: "If I had a Green Automobile/ I'd go find my old companion/ in his house on the Western ocean." 1980

► **Before collaborating** with Ginsberg on a lecture about the visionary poet William Blake at the Jack Kerouac School of Disembodied Poetics. 1980

► **When they first met,** Ginsberg claimed it was to tangle with Corso's verse. Gregory countered, "Man, you wanted my spirit. You didn't even know I wrote poetry." It's an argument that'll never be settled. 1980

▲ **Leading Naropa students** through William Blake's prophetic books, the
two teachers focus on the imagination. Blake's "tygers"—and his wish that all
God's children be prophets—reverberate in Ginsberg's work. 1980

"**Old moon my eyes** are new moon with human footprint..."—Allen Ginsberg, from "Poem Rocket," 1980

Poet Anne Waldman, author of *Fast Speaking Woman,* co-founded the Jack Kerouac School for Disembodied Poetics at Naropa Institute with Ginsberg. For many years they co-directed the school in Boulder, Colorado. 1981

Ginsberg's interest in meditation came out of his friendship with Gary Snyder, who studied Zen Buddhism in Japan. Allen was also inspired by a fateful meeting with Chögyam Trungpa, Rinpoche on the streets of New York in 1970; the Rinpoche later became his teacher. 1981

▲ **Drummond Hadley driving** Gary Snyder and Ginsberg to
a party in the Flatiron Mountains outside Boulder. 1981

▶ **Signaling Gary Snyder** that he plans to attend Snyder's meditation class later that morning. 108

▲ **"Thoughts Sitting Breathing"** by Ginsberg begins, "OM—the pride
of perfumed money, music food from China, a place to sit quiet…" 1981

▶ **Anne Waldman, Jack Collom,** Ginsberg, Robert Creeley, Larry
Fagin, Diane di Prima, Michael Brownstein, and Peter Orlovsky meet
for the mother of all poetry classes on a Boulder afternoon. 1981

▲ **Rapping poetics.** Ginsberg admired Creeley's quick mind and generosity toward his peers and younger writers. 1981

◄ **Anne Waldman takes center stage** making an "outrider" point. Robert Creeley often came to Naropa for the summer sessions. His early works showed a poetic economy much different than Ginsberg's longer, incantatory lines. 1981

No single book of poetry looms as large in Beat history as *Howl and Other Poems.* It communes with Blake, Whitman, and poets yet to come. 1981

A moment of solitude on the balcony of Buddhist Peter Goldfarb's home in Boulder. 1981

▲ **When William Burroughs met** the young Ginsberg in Greenwich Village, 1943, neither man knew that the other was a writer. Ginsberg worked tirelessly to see *Junky* and *Naked Lunch* into print. 1981

▶ **James Grauerholz, Burroughs's secretary,** and Allen look over a Burroughs manuscript before the novelist's reading at Naropa. Burroughs read that night in his dry, acerbic voice. 1981

◄ **Karel Appel and Ginsberg worked** together on this painting of Jack Kerouac. The collaboration marked the 25th anniversary of the publication of *On the Road*. 1982

▶ **A gathering of Kerouac's** colleagues—poets, novelists, artists, and itinerant prophets—at Naropa's salute to *On the Road*. Look for Burroughs, Ginsberg, John Clellon Holmes (author of *Go*), Jack Micheline, Robert Creeley, Abbie Hoffman, Paul Krassner, and Timothy Leary in the group. 1982

▶ **Two literary rebels reconnoiter** at the art exhibition during the Kerouac *On the Road* Conference at Naropa. 1982

◀ **Robert Frank's** The Americans remains a hallmark of post-World War II photography. Frank's 1959 film *Pull My Daisy*, set in New York, was a collaboration with Ginsberg, Kerouac, Corso, musician David Amram, *et. al.* 1982

▲ **Reminiscing.** Through nearly six decades they kept vigil over American culture. 1982

◀ **The incomprehensible is explained to the baffled.** Corso spins off a story looking at Burroughs' artwork during the *On the Road* exhibition in Boulder. 1982

▲ **To photograph Corso is a singular experience.** The introduction to Corso's *Gasoline*, published by City Lights in 1958, was written by Ginsberg. 1984

◀ **Back in San Francisco,** standing on the corner of Grant and Vallejo in North Beach, the "angel-headed hipsters" conspire to make the sidewalks sing. 1984

▲ **Poets Tisa Walden, Howard Hart, Gregory Corso,** Ginsberg, Jack Hirschman, and Sarah Menefee on the steps of Saint Francis of Assisi Church in North Beach. 1984

▶ **En route to China** with his newly-acquired medium-format camera, a gift from Berenice Abbott. 1984

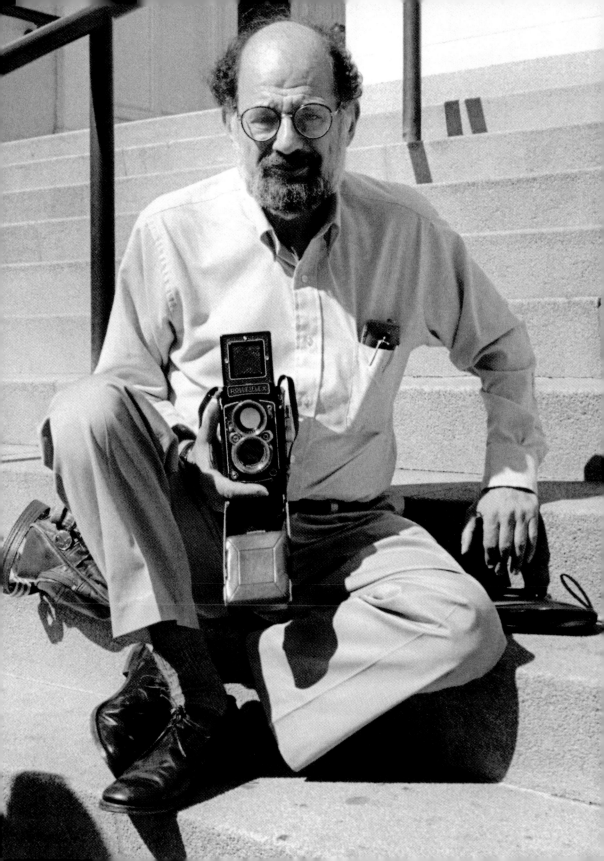

▶ **A troika of poets…**Ginsberg, Michael McClure, and Ferlinghetti before Ginsberg's reading from his *Collected Poems*. That night the small store could not hold the excited crowd waiting for a chance to hear America's bard. 1984

◀ **Ferlinghetti and** young admirers greet Ginsberg as he celebrates the publication of his *Collected Poems, 1947-1980* at City Lights Bookstore. 1984

◀ **Editing photos** in his New York digs with Carroll Terrell. He was constantly shuffling through archival material, making a living memory of the Beat experiment for future scholars and writers. 1985

▶ **The Twelfth Street apartment** was a library of the marvelous, filled with folders, books, filing cabinets, and photo albums. Ginsberg's papers are now archived at Stanford University's Special Collections Library. 1985

▲ **Norman Mailer addresses the PEN** Conference at the Plaza Hotel in Manhattan. 1985

◄ **"Sir spirit, forgive me my sins,**/ Sir spirit give me your blessing again,/ Sir Spirit forgive
my phantom body's demands…" —Allen Ginsberg, from "Elegy for Neal Cassady." 1985

▶ **Carl Solomon,** to whom "Howl" is dedicated, expounds. Solomon was instrumental in finding a publisher for Burroughs's *Junkie* in the early '50s and wrote two books of his own, *Mishaps* and *More Mishaps.* 1987

◀ **Gallerist Tony Shafrazi with guests of honor** Allen Ginsberg, William Burroughs, and Kurt Vonnegut at Burroughs' painting exhibition in Soho. 1993

▲ **Signing copies** of *Allen Ginsberg: Photographs*, a Twelvetrees Press edition, in the Poetry Room at City Lights. The book was a landmark for Ginsberg, leading to world-wide exhibitions of his photographs. 1990

▶ **With poet Andy Clausen at City Lights.** Outside the window the North Beach night is illuminated by neon and subterranean light. 1990

▲ **"A photograph is** sometimes just like a poem, capturing the seen and the unseen as well."—Allen Ginsberg. 1991

◀ **Two poets in profile** at the Gregory Corso/Taylor Mead poetry reading at Saint Marks Poetry Project in the Bowery, New York. 1991

▲ **Peter Orlovsky and editor Raymond Foye** in the foreground as Ginsberg snaps Herbert
Huncke, who is about to read from *The Beat Book* , edited by scholar Ann Charters. 1991

▶ **After a reading** in honor of Kerouac at the annual memorial in Lowell, Massachusetts,
the novelist's hometown. Ginsberg wrote in the dedication to *Howl:*, "For Jack Kerouac,
new Buddha of American prose, who spit forth intelligence into eleven books...." 1994

▲ **At the New York University Conference,** *The Beat Generation*, Allen takes in
Kerouac's mystic drawings, never before exhibited. This was a pivotal evening, the
first time his old writing colleague was honored by a major American university. 1994

▶ **Elaine de Kooning's portrait of Ginsberg** rests next to Kerouac's old paint
box and chair, which were brought to the *Beat Art* exhibition, part of the New
York University *Beat Generation* Conference, by curator Bernie Mindich. 1994

▲ **Meditating on Robert LaVigne's** 1954 painting of
Peter Orlovsky. "I had not met Peter yet, but the image
on canvas transfixed me."—Allen Ginsberg. 1994

◀ **Ferlinghetti and Ginsberg** study Harry Redl's famous 1957 *Evergreen Review*
portraits. Allen mused, "Wow! We looked so young back then." 1994

▲ **Ginsberg, Ferlinghetti, and Andrei Voznesensky** party after the New York University *Beat Generation* Conference. The famed Russian poet made a surprise visit. That night the audience experienced Voznesensky's hilarious "money poem." 1994

▶ **In Washington Square Park** with Voznesensky, poet of the dark Russian night. 1994

▲ **Russia's most famous living poet,** Andrei Voznesensky, backstage with Ray Manzarek and
Allen at the Town Hall reading for the New York University *Beat Generation* Conference. 1994

▲ **Making yet another immortal image** of the mortal Corso,
who maintained, "I will not know my own death." 1994

▲ **Besieged by media** at the dedication of the Allen Ginsberg Library on the Naropa Institute campus. He loved the thought of young poets finding inspiration while combing the shelves of this library in the Rockies. 1994

▶ **An interview with Ferlinghetti on Denver television.** Topics included the ongoing youth rebellion, new interest in the environment, and social activism. 1994

▲ **In front of the photo montage** *The Life and Times of Allen Ginsberg*
with curator Althea Cronford in the Boulder Public Library. 1994

▶ **Bobbie Louise Hawkins applauds the performance.** David Amram at the keyboard
during the opening celebration for *The Life and Times of Allen Ginsberg* photo exhibit. 1994

▲ **Robert Creeley, Cecil Taylor, and Allen** backstage before Taylor's solo performance at Naropa's Tribute to Ginsberg, Boulder, CO. Cecil Taylor's *oeuvre* revolutionized the boundaries of free jazz. 1994

◄ **Backstage with Philip Glass** before their performance of "Wichita Vortex Sutra," a '60s poem by Ginsberg set to music by Glass that foreshadows war and solitude among American youth. 1994

▲ **Rapping with David Amram** in Boulder about their
wild young lives in Manhattan, running with Kerouac,
and being haunted by his enigmatic vision. 1994

◄ **Performing "Wichita Vortex Sutra"** at the Naropa Tribute to Ginsberg. "All we
do is for this frightened thing/ we call Love, want and lack—" Ginsberg's onslaught of
images make the poem roll like a big-rig on the American highway. 1994

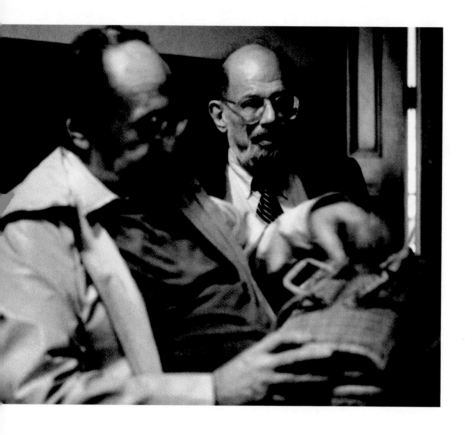

◀ **John Wieners and Ginsberg** watch Robert Creeley read in Lowell, Massachusetts, at the annual birthday celebration for Kerouac. Inside the basket are Kerouac artifacts Wieners brought from his Beacon Hill apartment for the festivities. 1994

▶ **David Amram accompanied Allen** at his first public appearance mixing music and poetry. In the '50s, Amram, Ginsberg, Kerouac, and Neal Cassady collaborated on the song "Pull My Daisy" for the 1959 Robert Frank and Alfred Leslie film. 1994

▲ **Jerry Brown at** the Berkeley benefit for Middle East Children's
Alliance. Brown was elected Mayor of Oakland in 1998; a three-
hour poetry event was held at his inauguration. 1994

◄ **Waiting in Berkeley** to be interviewed by poet Jack Foley for the "Cover to Cover"
KPFA radio program. A transcription was later published in *Poetry Flash*. 1994

◄ **Wavy Gravy** has been an underground figure since the late '50s, as beatnik poet-artist in Greenwich Village, then famed emcee at the Woodstock Festival. He's now known for Berkeley's Seva Foundation, fighting blindness in third world countries, and Camp Winnarainbow, where the art of clownmanship thrives. 1994

▶ **Andy Clausen, Bob Sharrard, and Ginsberg** escort Shig Murao to a waiting car after the benefit for Children's Alliance. Murao was the bookseller at City Lights when the police came with an arrest warrant for selling *Howl and Other Poems*. Shig and Allen remained lifelong friends. 1994

◀ **Reading from** a manuscript of new poems en route to Philip Whalen and the Hartford Zen Center, San Francisco. 1994

▶ **Reading poems** of William Carlos Williams with two young writers at a Haight Ashbury bookstore. The concept of "no idea but in things" helped form Ginsberg's poetics as a young man. Both poets wrote of Paterson, New Jersey, and Dr. Williams from nearby Rutherford. Williams included letters from the young Ginsberg in his five-book epic *Paterson*. 1994

▲ **Amiri Baraka at The Cooler's** "Free Mumia Abu Jamal" rally in Manhattan. Baraka is
the author of many books of poetry and prose, including *Preface to a Twenty Pound Suicide
Note*, the revolutionary play *The Dutchman*, and the classic study *Blues People*. 1995

▶ **Reading new poems** at The Cooler on 14th Street accompanied by Marc Ribot
of the Jazz Passengers—an inspired evening of poetry-jazz improvisation. 1995

▶ **Artist Francisco Clemente,** his wife
Alba, Ginsberg, and New York novelist
Tama Janowitz in the Whitney stairwell
at the opening of *Beat Culture and the
New America,* 1950-1965. 1995

◀ **Bruce Conner explains** his *assemblage* to Allen, Ray Manzarek, and Michael McClure at the Whitney Museum.
Conner's long association with the Beats underscores his own outsider persona. In the exhibit were works by
Wallace Berman and George Herms, contributors to *Semina*, an early journal of the arts in California. 1995

▶ **In concert with** Steven Taylor at the Whitney *Beat Culture and the New America* event. Whether performing William Blake poems set to music or Ginsberg's own works, these collaborators draw a line right back to Robert Burns. 1995

▲ **Investigative poet,** *Woodstock Journal* editor, and leading force of the '60s folk-rock band The Fugs, Ed Sanders in the Green Room before the Whitney *Beat Culture* perfomance. 1995

▲ **After performing** at the Whitney *Beat Culture* event, Ginsberg signs a copy of *The Nation* featuring his poem, "The Ballad of the Skeletons." It was the first political poem ever published by the magazine. "…Said the President Skeleton/ I won't sign the bill…Said the Speaker skeleton/ Yes you will…" 1995

◄ **Together for the last time** with McClure and Corso at the Whitney *Beat Culture* performance. 1995

◀ **Meeting Ramblin'** Jack Elliott after Ginsberg's last reading in San Francisco—October 12—at the de Young Museum's *Beat Culture and the New America* exhibition. In 1954, Jack Kerouac read the entire manuscript of *On the Road* to Elliott in one evening. A few years later Ramblin' Jack named an album *Kerouac's Dream*. 1996

▶ **Heading downtown** in a sleek limo with McClure after the Whitney opening, on the way to the party in Soho. 1995

▲ **Signing** *Cosmopolitan Greetings* for Nobel Laureate Czeslaw Milosz. 1996

◀ **The self-devouring snake** is called Uroboros, a symbol of continuity and primal unity. Allen often depicted this image in his dedications. Ginsberg would often draw a benign and smiling Buddha above the recipient's name. 1996

▲ **The *Poetry Flash* benefit** sponsored by City Arts and Lectures at the War
Memorial Opera House featured Czeslaw Milosz and Ginsberg. Filling out the bill
were U.S. Poet Laureate Bob Hass, Thom Gunn, Adrienne Rich, and Gary Snyder.
Ginsberg had just arrived on the red-eye from the Czech Republic. 1996

▶ **Gary Snyder,** winner of the Pulitzer Prize for *Turtle Island*, was one of Allen's
closest friends. For Ginsberg and Kerouac, this West Coast poet symbolized
the freedom and independence of the Western littoral. Snyder's study and
practice of Zen Buddhism blossomed into an ongoing poetics. 1996

◀ **In City Lights Bookstore,** on his way to lunch with Ferlinghetti, his longtime friend, fellow poet, and publisher. 1996

▶ **This is the last** picture of Allen Ginsberg at City Lights. The day is December 18, 1996.

▲ **Passers-by left small personal offerings** outside of Saint
Mark's Church in spontaneous tribute to the great poet. 1997

◄ **Peter Orlovsky in front of the altar** at Saint Mark's after Allen Ginsberg's Blakean memorial.
That night, April 12, the New York literary world came to a standstill to honor its most famous poet. 1997.

R.M.D.C.

In the half light of dawn
a few birds warble
under the Pleiades.

Allen Ginsberg

for Chris Felver
July 31, 1983

▶ **The Buddhist Jew** with a Tibetan lama's mind contemplating the brevity of epic poetry and the endlessness of haiku.

First Row

Abbie Hoffman

Anne Waldman

William Burroughs

Philip LaMantia

Gary Snyder

Second Row

Jack Micheline

Carl Solomon

Herbert Huncke

Robert Creeley

Tuli Kupferberg

Third Row

Diane DiPrima

Peter Orlovsky

Allen Ginsberg

Philip Whalen

Ted Joans

Fourth Row

Gregory Corso

Bobbie L. Hawkins

Bob Kaufman

Ed Sanders

Seymour Krim

Fifth Row

Michael McClure

Lawrance Ferlinghetti

Timothy Leary

Amiri Baraka

Harold Norse

Sixth Row

Cecil Taylor

John Weiners

Howard Hart

Ken Kesey

JoAnne Kyger